It buzzed a box.

The fly buzzed a boy
in the back.

"Shoo, fly!"

The fly buzzed a girl
in the back.

"Shoo, fly!"

The fly buzzed a boy
in the front.

"Shoo, fly!"

The fly buzzed a girl
in the front.

"Shoo, fly!"

The fly buzzed the driver.

The bus stopped.
"Shoo, fly!"

The box fell.

The lid fell off.
The fly buzzed the box.

"Snap," went a frog.

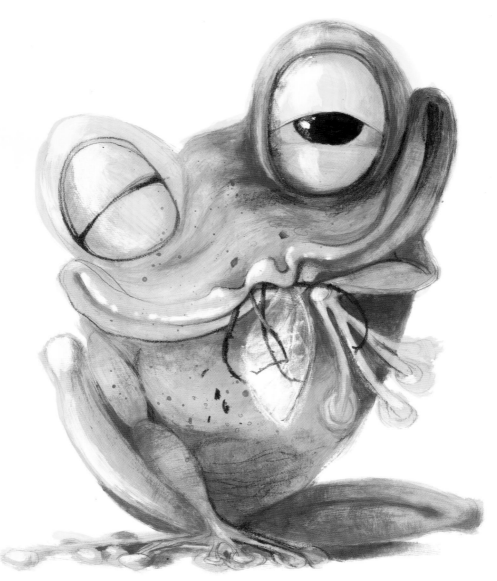